My First Visit to London

Rebecca Hunter

Photography by Chris Fairclough

≷ ⊖ **One Day Travelcard** No photocard required
Class
STD
Ticket type
TRAVELCARD
Price
Issue date
Status
CHILD 12 JLY
Valid on
Between
GODALMING
Zones
& R1256
Number
Valid
Route/also available at
Valid within zone(s) indicated
Valid off peak as advertised
Not for resale
Not valid on Night Buses

First Times
My First Day at School
My First School Play
My New Sister
My First Visit to Hospital
My New Dad
Moving House
My First Pet
My First Visit to London

Published by Evans Brothers Ltd
2A Portman Mansions
Chiltern Street
London W1M 1LE
England

Hunter, Rebecca
My first visit to London, - (First Times)
1. London (England) - Description and travel - Juvenile literature
1. Title
914.2'1'04859

ISBN 0 237 52145 8

Acknowledgements
Planning and production by Discovery Books
Editor: Rebecca Hunter
Photographer: Chris Fairclough
Designer: Ian Winton

The publishers would like to thank Hannah Vernon, Rosemary Vernon, Heather's Teddies and the London Transport Museum for their help in the preparation of this book, and Tim Humphrey for the use of the photograph on page 13.

Contents

We are going to London.

Mum and I are going to London. On the train we look at the map to plan our trip. At last we arrive at Waterloo Station.

This is the River Thames.

We look out over the River Thames to the Houses of Parliament and Big Ben.

Then we walk over Westminster Bridge.

We go to Buckingham Palace.

The Queen lives here at Buckingham Palace. The palace is huge and has over 600 rooms. The guards wear big, furry hats called bearskins.

I meet one of the guards.

These guards have different uniforms.

I like the guard on horseback. The horse is very well-behaved.

Trafalgar Square is full of pigeons.

We catch a red bus to Trafalgar Square. There are lots of pigeons and big statues of lions.

I buy a postcard.

The street stalls sell souvenirs. I buy a postcard to send to my Dad.

Covent Garden is fun.

We are looking at the stalls in Covent Garden market.

I like this bear best. He is dressed as a Beefeater.

We watch some jugglers.

After lunch we watch the street entertainers. I think these jugglers are really clever. They make me laugh.

This is the London Transport Museum.

We go to the London Transport Museum.

It has lots of old buses and trams.

Mum buys me a T-shirt.

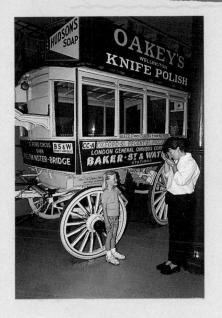

This carriage would have been pulled by horses 100 years ago.

Mum buys me a T-shirt with Tower Bridge on it. That is where we are going next.

We catch a river boat.

We walk down to the river to catch a river boat.

We go past the Tower of London. Mum says it is over 900 years old.

This is Tower Bridge.

We go under Tower Bridge.
When big ships go by, it has
to open up.

We see the Millennium Dome.

We get off the boat at Greenwich. We look at an old sailing ship called the Cutty Sark. We can also see the Millennium Dome.

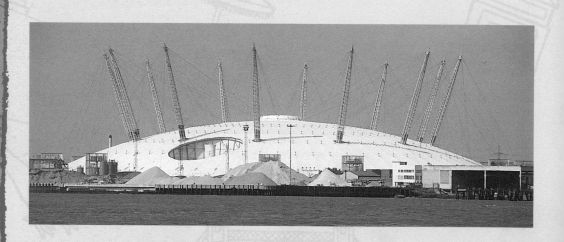

I am tired.

I would like to
see inside the
Dome but we
are going
home now.

I am very
tired but I
did enjoy my
first visit to
London.

Index

Map of our route

This is the map of our route.

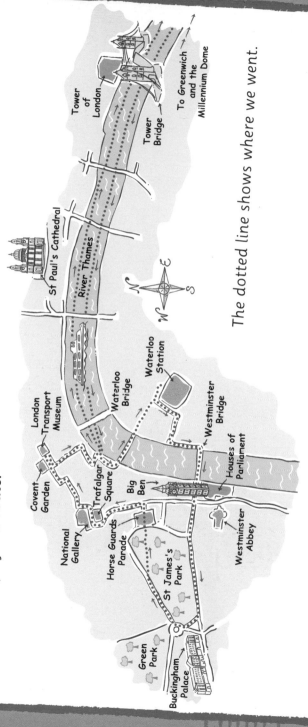

The dotted line shows where we went.